SOCRATES IN 90 MINUTES

Socrates
IN 90 MINUTES

Paul Strathern

IVAN R. DEE
CHICAGO

S

SOCRATES IN 90 MINUTES. Copyright © 1997 by Paul
Strathern. All rights reserved, including the right to reproduce
this book or portions thereof in any form. For information,
address: Ivan R. Dee, Inc., 1332 North Halsted Street, Chicago
60622. Manufactured in the United States of America and
printed on acid-free paper.

Library of Congress Cataloging-in-Publication Data:
Strathern, Paul, 1940–
    Socrates in 90 minutes / Paul Strathern.
      p. cm.
    Includes bibliographical references and index.
    ISBN 1–56663–147–5 (alk. paper). — ISBN 1–56663–148–3
(pbk. : alk. paper)
    1. Socrates.   2. Philosophers—Greece—Biography.
3. Philosophy, Ancient.   I. Title.
B316.S75   1997
183'.2—dc21
[B]   96–40322

Contents

SOCRATES IN 90 MINUTES

Introduction

In the beginning was the world, and we didn't really know much about it. But we survived regardless. The original philosopher was the puzzled Neolithic who questioned this state of affairs. What on earth was going on? What was it all about?

For countless millennia the answers we came up with were not philosophy. They consisted of superstition, fairy tales, and religion. The first people to come up with philosophical answers—that is, those who used reason and observation unclouded by metaphysical mumbo jumbo—were the ancient Greeks, in the sixth century B.C. Precisely why this major step in human evolution should have taken place at this time on the obscure shores of the Aegean remains a mystery. The Chinese, the Babylonians, and the ancient Egyptians were all more advanced at this stage, their civilizations more powerful and extensive. They also had superior practical technology and knew far more about mathematics. The intricacies of silk manufacture, pyramid building, and the ability to predict eclipses were well beyond Greek capacities. And compared with the theological sophistications of the Chinese, Babylonian, and ancient Egyptian religions, the ancient Greeks' collection of primitive myths about the behavior of the gods on Olympus was laughable. This was religion retarded in its infantile stage of development (only when it matures does religion require human sacrifice).

But this childish state of affairs may well hold the key to the mystery, at least in part. Without it, the miraculous flowering of ancient Greek culture—which is still recognizable as the foundation of Western culture—may never have occurred. The trivial religion of the Greeks had no place for theological or intellectual speculation. Before the Greeks, intellectual inquiry had always been related to religion—allowing metaphysics and superstition to infiltrate the processes of reason and observation. Babylonian astronomy was plagued by astrology; Egyptian mathematics was permeated with religious superstition. When the ancient Greeks began to ask intellectual questions, they were unencumbered by such ballast. Their thoughts soared free in a real world.

Perhaps as a result of this freedom, the development of ancient Greek culture took place at truly miraculous speed. For example, Greek tragedy developed from stilted and primitive religious ritual to sophisticated drama (formally little altered to this day) in the course of a *single generation*. Likewise, philosophy began midway through the sixth century B.C., but by the end of the following century it had produced Plato, whom many still regard as its most masterly exponent. The advances in ancient Greece during the fifth century B.C. remain qualitatively unrivaled to this day. And only the twentieth century exceeds it in quantitative change.

The first philosopher is generally recognized as Thales of Miletus, an ancient Greek from Asia Minor. We know he was practicing his profession in 585 B.C. because he achieved fame by predicting an eclipse of the sun which occurred in that year. (This knowledge he almost certainly cribbed from Babylonian sources.) Thales is regarded as the first real philosopher because he was the first to attempt an explanation of the world in terms of its observable nature rather than by mythology. This meant that his conclusions could be subjected to rational argument about whether they were right or wrong. The main thesis of Thales's philosophy was that everything was ultimately made up of water. He thus set the tone for all future philosophy by getting it wrong.

After Thales, philosophy rapidly began to flourish. More philosophers appeared, with a succession of different explanations of the world. It wasn't made of water, it was made of fire—then air, then pieces of light, and so on. The philosophers who belong to this period (mid-sixth to mid-fifth century B.C.) are generally

10

known as the pre-Socratics. For the most part only fragments of their philosophy remain—either in directly written form or in references from other sources. Despite this, many of their names are still familiar. Pythagoras—famous for the mathematical theorem he did not in fact discover himself—discerned the role played by numbers in music. (Harmony depends upon numerical ratios.) This led him to believe that the world is ultimately made up of numbers. Such a theory is not quite as daft as it may at first appear. Einstein, for instance, certainly believed that the universe could be explained in terms of mathematics. Modern scientists may not believe that the world is made up of numbers, but from quarks to quasars numbers play a central role in description and definition. Another pre-Socratic philosopher who anticipated modern science was Democritus, who believed the world was made up of atoms. (It was to be more than two thousand years before scientists came round to this point of view.)

Anaxagoras was the first Athenian philosopher—though it's almost certain he was originally an import, shipped in from Ionia (Asia Minor) by Pericles to raise the tone of Athenian education. Anaxagoras was very much a minor philosopher. He reversed the trend of explaining the world in terms of a single substance, claiming rather that it consisted of an infinite number of substances. Indeed, everything contained a bit of everything else. As a result of this mélange he was forced to argue that even plants had a mind of their own, that snow was partly black, and that water contained elements of dryness. Despite these anomalies masquerading as ideas, Anaxagoras is important. It was he who introduced philosophy to Athens, and he was also the man who introduced philosophy to Socrates. Anaxagoras was Socrates' teacher.

According to one source, Anaxagoras also taught Pericles, who went on to become the driving political force behind Athens's golden era (mid-440s B.C. to the end of the 430s B.C.). This period saw the construction of the Parthenon, the great era of Greek tragedy, the sculpture of Phidias (whose Zeus became one of the Seven Wonders of the Ancient World), and the emergence of classical philosophy with Socrates. What part (if any) Anaxagoras had in influencing Pericles is not known. What is known is that Anaxagoras claimed the sun was a huge superhot rock and the moon was made of earth. For expressing such ideas (ironically his only ones that came close to the truth) Anaxagoras was prosecuted for impiety and forced to flee Athens for his life. This is the first real evidence of philosophy being taken seriously. It was dangerous.

Anaxagoras first demonstrated these lessons to Socrates—that philosophy was both serious and dangerous. As we shall see, Socrates chose to ignore them. Ignoring the first lesson made him one of the most engaging of all philosophers. Ignoring the second was to cost him his life.

Just a century after it had begun, philosophy entered its greatest age. This was to include three of the finest philosophers the world has seen. The first of these was the idiosyncratic Socrates, who spent so much of his time talking about philosophy on the streets of Athens that he never actually got around to writing anything down.

This means that we know of Socrates' teaching only through the writings of his famous pupil Plato, and it's often difficult in these writings to determine which ideas are Plato's and which are those of his mentor.

Socrates developed a method of negatively aggressive questioning called dialectic (the forerunner of logic). This he used in conversation to cut through the twaddle of his adversaries and arrive at the truth. Plato captured the spirit of these conversations in his classic dialogues. Plato's more orthodox approach and way of life were to bring a much-needed element of respectability to philosophy. But he persisted in the philosophic tradition of getting it wrong. Plato believed that the real world was made up of ideas, and that the world we see and experience consists of no more than shadows. Despite this unrealistic attitude, many thinkers believe that all of philosophy since has been little more than footnotes to Plato's writing. Although this is an exaggeration, it's certainly true that Plato was the first to formulate clearly many of the basic

14

philosophical problems that exercise us to this day.

The third member of this triumvirate was Aristotle, who was one of Plato's pupils. The scholarly Aristotle firmly rejected his master's attempt to make philosophy interesting by presenting it in the form of dialogues. Instead he wrote scores of treatises, many of which were mislaid by his ungrateful followers. Aristotle's rules of thought and classification laid the foundations for most philosophical and scientific thought during the next two millennia. Only in recent centuries have we begun to appreciate *how* Aristotle got it wrong. He appears to have understood that all comprehensive explanations were bound in the end to be wrong—but this didn't stop him from trying for one.

Without philosophy, which began in ancient Greece and for centuries retained its distinctive Greek character, we would not be what we are today. We would have no science, and the attempt to arrive at truth of any sort would remain largely a matter of fantasy and whim—just as it remains in the so-called sciences of politics, psychology, and economics, for instance. Even ethics continues to languish in this sad state, despite the persistent attentions of philosophers and theologians through the ages. Nowadays we are not only no better, morally speaking, than we were more than two thousand years ago, but we don't even know how to be.

It has taken philosophers twenty-five centuries of getting it wrong to conclude that getting it wrong isn't the point. Now they believe that the mere practice of philosophy is what matters. Thus philosophy has become an activity, like wine-tasting or tax evasion, with similarly ambiguous effects on the practitioner. For the first time in the history of philosophy, the attempt by any individual to construct a philosophy as such (that is, one of his own) has become redundant. The tradition of Plato, Kant, Ehrensvard, and Wittgenstein has come to an end. This tradition of reason and observation, which attracted some of the finest minds the world has known, first grew to maturity with Socrates.

Socrates' Life and Works

Socrates was born in 469 B.C. in a village on the slopes of Mount Lycabettus, which was then a twenty-minute walk from Athens. His father was a sculptor and his mother a midwife. Initially the young Socrates was apprenticed to his father; according to one tradition, he worked on *The Three Muses in Their Habits* which adorned the Acropolis. He was then sent to study with Anaxagoras.

Socrates went on to study under the philosopher Archelaus, "by whom he was beloved in the worst sense," according to Diogenes Laertius, the third-century A.D. biographer. In ancient Greece, as still in much of the eastern Mediterranean, homosexuality was regarded as a quite acceptable diversion. Not until the advent of Christianity was a limited heterodox approach to replace such orthodox sexual practice. So while Anaxagoras was forced to flee Athens in fear of his life for teaching his pupils that the sun was a radiant star, Archelaus remained free to indulge in more than intellectual intercourse with his pupils.

With Archelaus, Socrates studied mathematics and astronomy as well as the teachings of earlier philosophers. Philosophy had been pursued for just over a century and was very much the nuclear physics of the age. Indeed, the world of philosophy (which consisted entirely of water, then fire, then points of light, and so on) bore as much relation to the real world as the world of modern nuclear physics bears to our own everyday reality. We scarcely regard our encounters with mesons as the highlight of our daily existence, and one suspects that the ancient Greeks had a similarly blasé attitude toward the latest revelation that their world was in fact a goldfish bowl, a furnace, or a fireworks display.

Socrates soon decided that these ~~speculations about the nature of the world were of no possible benefit to humanity~~. For an ostensibly reasonable thinker, Socrates was curiously antiscientific. Here he was almost certainly ~~influenced by~~ one of the greatest pre-Socratic philosophers, ~~Parmenides of Elea~~. During his youth Socrates is said to have met the aging Parmenides and "learned much from him." ~~Parmenides resolved the conflict between those who believed the world was made up of a single substance (such as water or fire) and those like Anaxagoras who believed it consisted of a great many substances.~~ He overcame this conflict by the simple method of ignoring it. ~~According to Parmenides, the world as we know it is merely an illusion.~~ It doesn't matter how many things we think it is made of, because it doesn't exist. ~~The only true reality consists of eternal Being,~~ which is ~~infinite, unchanging,~~ and ~~indivisible.~~ For this Being there is ~~no past and no future~~: it subsumes the entire universe and everything that can possibly happen in it. "~~All is one~~" was ~~Parmenides' basic principle.~~ The ever-changing multiplicity we observe is merely the *appearance* of this static, all-embracing Being. Such an attitude to the world is scarcely favorable to science. Why bother with the workings of the world when they are nothing but an illusion?

In these early days philosophy was considered the study of all knowledge. (In Greek, philosopher means "lover of wisdom.") Mathematics, science, and cosmology did not exist *as such*; for centuries they were considered part of philosophy. As late as the seventeenth century Newton called his masterpiece on gravity and the workings of the universe *Philosophicae Naturalis Principia Mathematica* (*The Mathematical Principles of Natural Philosophy*). Only through the years did philosophy come to be regarded by many as the study of metaphysical—and thus unanswerable—questions. Whenever philosophy actually found the answers to questions, it ceased to be philosophy and became something else—a separate subject such as mathematics or physics. The most recent example of this is usually considered to be psychiatry, which claimed to answer a number of questions and immedi-

~~ately set up shop as a separate science.~~ (In fact it does not fulfill the philosophic requirements of a science, which demand a set of principles that can be tested by experiment—requirements not fulfilled by the inexactitudes of paranoia, psychoanalytic cures for dementia, and other forms of psychopathic disorder.)

In Socrates' time this entire field was of course considered part of philosophy (and philosophers were popularly regarded by the citizens of Athens much as the public today regards psychiatrists). Socrates' attitude toward philosophy was certainly psychological in the original sense of the word. (~~In Greek, psychology means "the study of the mind."~~) But he was no scientist. The influence of Parmenides saw to that. Reality was an illusion. This had a negative effect on Socrates and his successor Plato. During their lifetimes a few significant advances were made in mathematics, but only because this was considered timeless and abstract, and thus thought to be in some way connected with the ultimate reality of Being. Fortunately their successor Aristotle had a different attitude toward the world. He became in many ways the founder of science, and drew philosophy back toward reality. But the unscientific—indeed, antiscientific—attitude that developed with Socrates was to cast a blight on philosophy for centuries to come.

Largely as a result of Socrates' antiscientific attitude, the few great scientific minds of the ancient Greek world worked outside philosophy. Archimedes (in physics), Hippocrates (in medicine), and to a certain extent Euclid (in geometry) were isolated from philosophy and thus from any developing tradition of knowledge and argument. Ancient Greek scientists knew the earth went around the sun, knew it was round, and even calculated its circumference. They observed electricity and were aware that the earth had a magnetic field. Outside the "universal wisdom" of philosophy, such factual bits of knowledge were isolated to the status of oddities. We owe a great deal to Socrates for placing philosophy on the sound basis of reason. But the fact that philosophy came of age under the aegis of an antiscientist must count as one of the great misfortunes of human learning. It is difficult to overemphasize the significance of this missed opportunity. The mental energy expended in the Middle Ages calculating the number of angels who could stand on the head of a pin might instead have been dealing with the atoms first posited by Democritus.

Rather than questioning the world, Socrates believed we would be better off questioning ourselves. He adopted the celebrated maxim *"Gnothi seauton"*—Know thyself. (This saying is sometimes erroneously attributed to Socrates. In fact it may well have been coined by the first philosopher of all, Thales; it is also known to have been inscribed at the Delphic Oracle.)

Socrates began expounding his philosophy in the Agora, the marketplace of ancient Athens, whose extensive ruins are still visible beneath the Acropolis. Socrates' favorite spot here was the Stoa of Zeus Eleutherios, a shady colonnade lined with stallholders selling wares. The stone foundations of this stoa can still be traced quite plainly. They are truncated at their northern end by the busy Athens-Piraeus metro, and from beyond the nearby wire fence the calm of the ruins is shattered by the clamoring throng, blaring bouzouki tapes, and bawling stallholders of the Monastiraki flea market. All this cannot be very different from the uproar that must have prevailed in Socrates' day. We have to imagine Socrates conducting his philosophic business amidst the ancient equivalent of haggling jeans merchants, ghetto blasters blaring "Zorba the Greek," and the plaintive cries of peanut vendors. Yet in spite of this, someone must have actually heard what he had to say. And the young Socrates must have caused a stir in Athens, for by the time he was thirty the Delphic Oracle pronounced him the wisest of men.

Socrates said he found this difficult to believe, disingenuously claiming that "I know nothing except the fact of my own ignorance." In order to discover whether there was any truth in the oracle's pronouncement, Socrates set about questioning the other wise men of Athens, trying to discover what they knew. Socrates was a past master at exposing cant and erroneous beliefs. He would claim he knew nothing, and demand of his adversary precisely what it was that he knew. While his adversary explained, Socrates would prick the bubble of his illusions by asking pointed questions. Not for nothing did Socrates become known as "the gadfly of Athens." But his method of questioning was much more profound than it often at first appeared. Socrates would seek to clarify the debate by starting from first principles. This meant defining the basic concepts upon which his adversary's ideas rested, exposing inconsistencies, and particularly pointing out the consequences of such ideas. But Socrates also had a keen eye for human absurdity and was not above reducing his adversary to a laughingstock. Judging from all accounts, he must have been an infuriating conversational opponent—slippery, brilliant, and devious. And there's no doubt that this smart-aleck aspect of Socrates' character earned him more than a few enemies as well as gaining him a popular following among the iconoclastic youth of his day.

It wasn't long before Socrates had demonstrated to his own satisfaction that the so-called wise men of Athens in fact knew nothing—just like him. So he concluded that the Delphic Oracle had been right: he *was* the wisest man—because he *knew* that he knew nothing.

Socrates may have been rational and iconoclastic in his approach, but in certain ways he remained very much a creature of his age. Despite all the banter, Socrates seems to have believed that the Delphic Oracle spoke with the voice of the gods. He also firmly believed that "the soul is immortal and imperishable, and after death our souls continue to exist in another world." Although most of the time he held little truck with superstitious reverence for the gods and the soap opera of their mythology, he certainly believed there was a god of some sort. The reason he gave for this was that everyone appeared to believe in a god of some sort—a curious reason coming from someone who spent his life trying to disabuse people of erroneous thought processes.

But Socrates' philosophy was not all concerned with thought processes and analytical method. It also put forward a number of positive proposals—which means he may well have had to endure a taste of his own critical medicine on occasion. In Plato's dialogue *The Phaedo*, the character Socrates puts forward a Theory of Forms. Many consider this to be Plato's own theory, which he is merely expressing through the mouthpiece of Socrates. But when Plato wrote *The Phaedo* all the other characters who appear in this dialogue were still alive. It can thus be assumed that unless Plato wished to spend a lot of his time in the courts, the views put forward by these characters are what they actually believed. And as such they are likely to have discussed them with the actual Socrates. Having based so much of the dialogue on factual sources, it seems unlikely that Plato would then have introduced a fictitious Socrates spouting views he never held. Plato also stresses that Socrates "frequently put forward these values." Despite such evidence, the Theory of Forms is usually attributed to Plato.

All this goes to show the difficulty of attributing *anything* to someone who doesn't write anything down (perhaps one reason why so many of us cleverly adopt this ploy). One thing *is* certain about the Theory of Forms: neither Socrates nor Plato was the first to think of it. This feat is generally credited to Pythagoras. As we have seen, Pythagoras's studies of musical harmony led him to believe that the world was ultimately made up of numbers. But Pythagoras's conception of numbers was in many ways closer to our notion of form. According to Pythagoras, these abstractions (number, form) were the ultimate reality. They were the changeless abstract ideas from which the concrete, everchanging particulars of the world were formed. (As is evident, this also echoes Parmenides' idea of the ultimate reality consisting of Being, the ultimate entity that gives rise to the bits and pieces of our illusory world.)

In *The Phaedo* Socrates describes the nature of the world of forms (or numbers, or ideas. The Greek word he uses is *eidos*. This is the generic root of our word idea, and it can variously be translated as form, idea, or figure— where the notion of number and form actually coincide). According to Socrates, the world of forms is not accessible to our senses, only to

28

thought. We can think of such ideas as roundness and redness, but we do not perceive them. We only perceive a particular red ball. This is created out of the ideas of redness, roundness, elasticity, and so on. But how is this done? According to Socrates, particular objects receive their qualities by "participating" in the ideas from which they derive. One way of explaining this is to use the image of a plaster cast being made out of a mold. The abstract forms or ideas, the mold, give the particular object its shape, size, and other qualities.

The world of forms is the only real world, and is universal. It is the ultimate world in which all particular things participate. This world of forms has a hierarchy which rises to a peak in such universal ideas as Good, Beauty, and Truth. The qualities of goodness, beauty, and truth that we become aware of in particular objects lead us to contemplate these universal ideas in their abstract realm. This is a mystical attitude toward the world. It echoes the Indian thought from which it may well ultimately have derived— where the world is seen as the illusory veil of

Maya, which to the good man is transparent. For Socrates, these universal ideas are seen as superior to the world which first causes us to become aware of them.

Fortunately such a woolly system of thought, which scorns the particularity of the world we inhabit, is not entirely without precision. Number being synonymous with these higher ideas, the study of number becomes a superior pursuit. Thus mathematics was viewed by the Greeks as an enlightening activity, though only in its pure form. Calculating the sum of the angles of a polygon was quite acceptable; working out the number of buckets needed to fill a tank of water was definitely infra dig. This would have been *practical*—that is, it might have proved useful in the grubby world of particulars which we are forced to inhabit. Inevitably such an attitude viewed science as beyond the pale. This attitude was to persist throughout Western culture, and elements of it are still detectable even today.

Socrates grew up in the age of Pericles, when Athens was the strongest and most civilized city-state in the Hellenic world. Its advances influenced the entire course of human development. Besides its more concrete monuments, this era also witnessed the flowering of democracy as well as the consolidation of genuine mathematical and scientific thinking. And with Socrates it marked the coming of age of philosophy.

The era of comparative peace that had marked the Periclean Age came to an end with the outbreak of the Peloponnesian War in 431 B.C. This ruinous struggle between the quasi-democratic naval empire of Athens and philistine, militaristic Sparta continued for more than a quarter of a century. The war and its political repercussions played a continuing and crucial role in Socrates' life. It is worth remembering that what now appears to us as boringly sane and reasonable in his philosophy was conceived against an ever-changing background of bigotry, chicanery, and fear. Socrates' search for personal truth was conducted in an age of changing values and ebbing certainties whose moral climate we would find all too recognizable.

Upon the outbreak of the Peloponnesian War, Socrates was called to service as a hoplite (private, third class, with shield and sword). There are many conflicting accounts of Socrates' life, but one thing everyone seems to agree upon is his appearance. Socrates was one of the ugliest men in Athens. He had spindly bow legs, a paunch, his shoulders and neck were hairy, and he was bald (his pate was said to be "nobbly"). He was also famous for his broad snub nose, bulging eyes, and protruding lips.

Socrates not only looked like a philosopher, he dressed like one. Winter and summer he invariably wore the same shabby tunic together with a threadbare half-length cloak, and no matter the weather he always went about barefoot. According to his colleague Antiphon the Sophist, "A slave made to live in this fashion would have run away." Yet despite all this Socrates was apparently a good fighting soldier.

Ugly opinionated intellectuals are not usually popular in the ranks, but Socrates was such an oddball that he evidently intrigued his fellow soldiers. He took part in the siege of Potidaea in northern Greece, where it can get very cold in winter when the north wind whistles down from the Bulgarian mountains. In winter the ancient Greek armies became a motley bunch wrapped in all manner of skins, with pieces of felt tied around their feet—a far cry from the lithe naked youths one sees daintily fighting on Greek vases. Socrates' fellow soldiers would watch in amazement as he turned up on parade in the snow and ice in his bare feet, skimpy shift, and holey cloak.

But what particularly intrigued Socrates' fellow conscripts was the sight of him "thinking." According to Alcibiades, who served on the Potidaea campaign with Socrates, one day the philosopher awoke early and set about pondering a particularly difficult problem. For hours his companions watched as he stood in contemplative pose on a nearby patch of ground, completely lost to the world. At dinnertime he was still there. By now a number of his compatriots had become so intrigued that they decided to sleep outside their tents, just to see how long Socrates could keep up this performance. In the end he went on thinking throughout the night until the following dawn. Then he came to, offered a prayer to the coming day, and went about his business as if nothing had happened.

This is just one of several stories concerning Socrates' ability to lapse into a deep trance, and it has prompted a number of commentators to suspect that he suffered from a form of catalepsy. With other evidence that speaks of him hearing "voices," this might cause us to have suspicions about his sanity. Yet so much else we know about Socrates speaks of extreme common sense and levelheadedness. Indeed his philosophy sometimes appears to be little more than brilliantly applied common sense, spiced with a bit of native ironic cunning.

But the man capable of drifting into a trance while all about him were enduring the rigors of military boredom was also capable of great bravery when the occasion arose. According to Alcibiades, Socrates once noticed him lying wounded in the midst of a battle, slung him over his shoulder, and proceeded to carry him through a mass of armed enemy soldiers, thus saving his life.

Plato recounts how the young Alcibiades once fell in love with Socrates. This is difficult to imagine, and one can only assume that Alcibiades suffered from defective eyesight, though no mention is made of this. In Alcibiades' words: "When I heard his voice, my heart beat as if I was in a state of religious ecstasy." These sound much like the words of an impressionable youth enraptured by Socrates' wisdom. But no. In a passage much appreciated by classical scholars (and much censored by their masters), Alcibiades goes on to describe how he attempted to seduce Socrates.

First Alcibiades arranged to spend all day alone with Socrates, in the hope that their conversation might at some stage turn to "the subjects that a lover usually addresses to his darling when they are on their own together." But Socrates stuck to philosophy. Next Alcibiades asked Socrates to come with him to the gymnasium, so they could train together. In those days most athletic activities took place in the nude, so Alcibiades must have thought things were looking good when Socrates accepted his invitation.

Until one pauses for a moment to imagine how the bald, paunchy, spindle-legged Socrates must have looked stripped to the buff for action in the gym. Apparently undiscouraged by this romantically disillusioning sight, Alcibiades even managed to have a wrestling match with Socrates when there was no one else about. Still nothing happened.

Finally Alcibiades decided to invite Socrates to dinner at his house and get him drunk. He didn't succeed in getting Socrates drunk (no one ever managed this, no matter how much drink he downed), but he kept Socrates up so late that in the end he had to stay for the night. And in Alcibiades' words (according to Plato): "So he finally settled down on the couch he had used at dinner, right next to mine, and there was nobody else in the room but us." Under cover of darkness Alcibiades crept up beside Socrates and put his arms around him. But Socrates still wasn't willing, and in the end they fell asleep in each others arms "like brothers." By the mores of the time, Socrates' ability to resist the advances of a good-looking young man like Alcibiades was regarded as almost superhuman restraint.

Socrates was no ascetic—both his appearance and other historical evidence point against this. Yet he hardly lived the good life. He was constantly broke because he refused to work. He insisted upon devoting all his time to his god-given task—demonstrating to the citizens of Athens the profundity of their ignorance. But he appears to have received a minimal legacy from his father and was well looked after by his influential friends who often invited him to dinner. Socrates was evidently a highly entertaining guest at dinner parties, was willing to stay up chatting till dawn, and was capable of out-drinking everyone else. These dinner parties were usually all-male affairs but not homosexual events. Heterae (courtesans) were sometimes introduced, and Socrates seems to have enjoyed his fair share of whatever else was going free besides the food and drink.

According to Diogenes Laertius, Socrates spent part of his time conducting informal conversation classes with groups of young students. These were held at the shop of a certain Simon the Cobbler, by the boundary stone of the Agora. At the edge of the Agora you can still see the Horos, inscribed "I am the boundary stone of the Agora," which stands beside the wall of a small ancient dwelling. Recent excavations by this wall uncovered a large scattering of hobnails and a fifth-century B.C. cup inscribed with the name Simon. Miraculously, what had been discovered was the very shop where Socrates taught.

A few years ago when I was in Athens I visited this spot. I measured the foundations and found they were only four paces square. It must have been quite a crush inside, with Simon hammering away in the background and the occasional customer passing in and out, doubtless passing the odd witty comment. Teaching under such circumstances would have required quick-wittedness and the ability to hold an audience, two attributes that philosophers appear to have long since dispensed with. Socrates had the talents of a performer. And whatever else may be said of him, he always put on a good show. He remains the great alternative comedian of philosophy.

What exactly did Socrates teach at these lessons? One of his best-remembered remarks is, "The unexamined life is not worth living." This is very much the attitude of an intellectual with time on his hands. The Greek city-states were probably the first societies to produce something resembling an intellectual middle class with a degree of independence (due to democracy) and a degree of leisure (due to slavery). The Greeks had time to pursue their thoughts for their own sake and arrive at their own conclusions. Original thought of any kind requires idleness—a fact often overlooked by earnest, industrious mediocrities.

Socrates believed that a person's true self was his soul (psyche). Earlier philosophers had said that the soul was the eternal "breath of life" in us, which "sleeps while the body is active, but wakes while the body sleeps"—a kind of immortal subconscious, not too dissimilar from present-day Jungian doctrine. Socrates saw the soul as being much more like the *conscious* personality: an entity that could be judged clever or stupid, good or bad—that is, something for which we are morally responsible. He believed we should try to make our soul as good as possible, in order to make it like God.

But why? Socrates argued that all people seek happiness. Whether they achieve it or not depends upon the state of their soul. Only good souls achieve happiness. The reason why people are not good is because they are attracted to things that appear to be good but are not really good at all. If only we knew what was really good, we would always behave properly. Then there would be no conflict, either within ourselves or in society. Perhaps only a philosopher could be so naive as to believe this. It is just possible to argue that we do all share some hazy unexamined notion of good. But as soon as we begin to examine it, reducing it to practical particulars, we find we disagree—both individually and socially. Is it good to spend your time thinking about philosophy? Is it good to deprive women of the vote?

The Greeks lived in small city-states, a situation that promoted consensus. Athens, the most powerful of the ancient Greek city-states, had a free adult male population of 42,000 during this period. The Greeks also firmly believed in moderation. (Another celebrated maxim carved in stone at the Delphic Oracle was: "Nothing too much.") Socrates' idea of good would seem to be very much a product of his circumstances and his era. The total population of Athens during this period—including women, children, foreigners, and slaves—was probably around 250,000. Whether the disfranchised majority in Athens believed they were unhappy because of the bad state of their souls is a different matter.

At the age of fifty Socrates married Xanthippe. Chauvinist history paints Xanthippe as a shrew, but life with Socrates cannot have been easy. Imagine living with someone who spent his days arguing in the streets and never earned a penny, who came back at all hours after drinking with his friends (still with no money), and like all philosophers was an object of public ridicule throughout the neighborhood. (In the largest collection of contemporary Athenian jokes which has come down to us, almost a quarter feature a philosopher as the fall guy.)

Xanthippe is credited with being the only person who could get the better of Socrates in an argument. Yet, as is often the case in such stormy relationships, the evidence suggests that Socrates and Xanthippe were very close. She had three sons by him, none of whom appears to have learned much from his father. (According to all reports, they lived normal lives.) Despite Xanthippe's nagging and disapproval of her husband's behavior, she appears to have been fully aware that she was married to an exceptional human being. She stood by him unquestioningly in his time of need and was deeply moved at his death.

When Socrates was sixty-five, the Peloponnesian War finally ended in humiliation for Athens. The victorious Spartan leader Lysander sailed into Piraeus to supervise the establishment of a government sympathetic to Sparta, and installed the Thirty Tyrants. There followed a period of terror, with summary arrests, trials, and the confiscation of political opponents' property. Many of those who believed in democratic rule fled Athens, but Socrates remained. Surprisingly, despite his indomitable individualism, Socrates was not a democrat. Democracy as a form of government was still in its infancy and, unlike nowadays in its more mature form, was capable of both crass incompetence and excess. In Athens even the generals had been elected by popular ballot—and this method had proved even less effective than our present method of recruiting them from among army officers. The democrats were blamed by many for the disastrous conduct of the war, which had now reduced Athens to its knees. But Socrates argued against democracy on philosophic grounds, consistent with his ethical theory. He maintained that most people remained unhappy souls, unaware of the true good. As such they were liable to vote into power leaders who also had a mistaken idea about the good. This—and his view that there was only one ultimate good, which could only be discovered through his philosophy—was to lead him into dangerous waters.

When Plato later developed these ideas in his utopian *Republic*, the society he came up with was a nightmare. Like Plato (and Socrates), both the Soviets and the Nazis believed that there was only one ultimate good, which could only be discovered through their philosophy.

One of the leaders of the Thirty Tyrants was Critias, a former pupil of Socrates. But Critias soon made it clear that he had put the follies of his youth, such as education, behind him. Not that he had forgotten Socrates. Far from it. When Critias issued an edict forbidding the teaching of philosophy on the streets of Athens, he specifically mentioned Socrates. Critias knew only too well how his old teacher was capable of twisting the meaning of words to his own advantage, and he was in no mood for this kind of tomfoolery. The activity pursued by Socrates, no matter whether he called it philosophy or not, was expressly forbidden.

Some chose to see Socrates' decision to remain in Athens as evidence of his acquiescence to the rule of the Tyrants. But during the state of virtual civil war that followed, Socrates made it plain that he had no wish to take part in politics—he insisted upon remaining a man of principle.

Yet in fifth-century B.C. Athens it was virtually impossible to take no part in politics (unless you were a woman or a slave). The Tyrants were well aware of the invidiousness of their position and were keen to involve as many people as possible in their reign of terror, in order to spread their guilt. As a well-known man of principle, Socrates was an obvious candidate. One day, along with four others, he was summoned by the Tyrants and ordered to carry out a commission for them. He was to travel to the island of Salamis and arrest Leon, a leading member of the democratic opposition. This arrest was illegal, and Leon would almost certainly have been murdered as soon as he was brought to Athens. Regardless of the consequences, Socrates ignored his illegal orders and simply returned home. This decision would probably have cost Socrates his life but for a series of unforeseen developments: Critias was killed, and shortly afterward the Thirty Tyrants were deposed.

The Tyrants were replaced by democrats, who in turn also had it in for Socrates. But in order to heal the wounds of the civil war a general amnesty was declared, and Socrates was safe. Or so it appeared. In 399 B.C. he was arrested on charges of impiety and corruption of the young. The man behind these charges was a leading democrat named Anytus, who held a long-standing grudge against Socrates. Several years earlier Anytus's son had become a pupil of Socrates and had soon been persuaded by his teacher that he was better off living the "philosophical life" than going into the family tanning business.

The charges against Socrates were an obvious sham, but they involved the death penalty. This seems a bit excessive. Socrates was certainly unpopular, like any intellectual who argues for unpopular causes on grounds of principle. But the death penalty? For a seventy-year-old man? There remains a certain mystery about these charges and the consequent proceedings, and it seems unlikely they will ever be fully explained. I say mystery rather than secret, for it seems pretty obvious that everyone in Athens knew what the affair was really about.

Socrates stood trial before the five hundred members of the ruling council, each chosen at random from among the free men of Athens. The case against Socrates was brought by Meletus, who was merely a front man for Anytus. Meletus was an unsuccessful young tragic poet with long hair, a thin beard, and a beaky nose. He had a cutting, sarcastic way with words: a suitable adversary for the wily old Socrates.

Meletus put the case for the prosecution, ending with a demand for the death penalty.

It was now up to the accused to defend himself. Here Socrates seems to have misjudged the seriousness of the situation, and he began treating the court as if it were taking part in one of his philosophical conversation classes.

Some of the council were amused, but many were not. In the end the vote went against Socrates—280 to 220 in favor of the death penalty.

It was now up to Socrates to put forward a counterproposal for a lesser sentence. Still he refused to take the trial seriously. The charges against him were ludicrous, and he knew it. Socrates suggested that instead of being punished, he should in fact be honored for all he had done for the city. Instead of the death penalty he should be granted a place at the Prytaneum, the sacred hall where Athenian heroes were given free board at the public expense.

Uproar in court.

Acknowledging this outrage, Socrates demurred. He proposed that instead he should pay a fine, one commensurate with what he could afford. He suggested the derisory sum of one mina (enough to buy a pitcher of wine).

Further uproar. Socrates' friends were now begging him to come to his senses. Reluctantly Socrates proposed that instead of the death penalty he should be fined thirty mina.

By now the council had had enough. This time they returned a verdict of 360 to 140 in favor of the death penalty.

There is more than a hint of pigheadedness in Socrates' attitude to all this. Did he seriously believe the court would "recognize his worth" and release him? Or was he determined to die? (Had he suggested a sentence of exile, the court would certainly have agreed; and Socrates would have been comfortably supported in exile by his friends.) It would appear that Socrates harbored a desire for martyrdom, if only subconsciously.

Socrates should have been taken from the court and his sentence carried out forthwith. But on the day before the trial the sacred galley had set out on its annual voyage to the island of Delos, more than a hundred miles away across the Aegean. No executions were permitted until its return. So Socrates was manacled and taken to the state prison.

The precise outlines of this prison may still be seen, one hundred yards southwest of the present ruins of the Agora, amidst a patch of uneven waste ground littered with ancient stones and old foundations. The cell and inner bathhouse where Socrates was confined are directly on the right as one enters, and it was here that he received his friends during his last days. On this insignificant piece of earth (six paces by six paces) occurred the scenes described by Plato in his finest dialogues, masterpieces of ancient Greek literature worthy of comparison to Homer and the tragedies.

The hero of these dialogues remains himself throughout—utterly human, wise, and infuriatingly admirable, much as one imagines he intended. At one stage his friend Crito explains that he has hatched a plot for his escape, bribing the guards to turn a blind eye. But Socrates will have none of this. It would be contrary to everything he stands for. Socrates believed steadfastly in the rule of law, even when it was wrong.

Finally news arrives that the sacred galley has been sighted rounding Cape Sounion. It will soon be in Athens. Socrates' friends, and his wife Xanthippe, gather in his cell. Socrates then sends Xanthippe away because he wants no upsetting displays of emotion. As she leaves, Xanthippe protests, "But you're innocent!"

Characteristically Socrates replies, "Would you rather I was guilty?"

Socrates discusses with his friends (disciples would be a more apt description at this juncture) the nature of death and immortality. This is rendered in deeply moving detail by Plato, even though he was not there. (On this of all days, Plato was confined to bed with a fever.) Then Socrates is handed the bowl containing the hemlock. (Athens operated a do-it-yourself execution policy.) True to the end, Socrates pleads ignorance, asking, "What is the proper way to do this?"

"Just drink it down," replies the servant. "Then walk about until your legs feel weak. After that lie down, and the poison will do the rest."

"Am I allowed to pour a libation to the gods?"

"No. Don't spill any, or there may not be enough for the poison to work properly."

Socrates downs the bowl in one draft.

His friends are no longer able to disguise their grief and begin weeping uncontrollably.

Socrates admonishes them. "Pull yourselves together. Didn't I send Xanthippe away to avoid this kind of scene?"

He lies down, and slowly the numbness creeps up his body.

"Remember, Crito, I owe a cock to Asclepios," are his final words.

Then the gadfly of Athens is dead.

Socrates' last words, as recorded by Plato, have the ring of authenticity. Not least because it is not precisely clear what they mean. Here we can be fairly certain that truth triumphed over literature (even if Plato did have to rely on the hearsay of his friends).

Inevitably Socrates' last words have been subjected to various explanations. The most obvious is that Socrates simply owed a chicken to a friend named Asclepios, and wished to pay off his debt. But this is far too banal for many scholars. Asclepios, besides being a fairly common name, was also the god of medicine and healing. (He was usually depicted walking with a staff, entwined with a snake: the origin of the emblem that adorns pharmacies and ambulances to this day.) Some suggest that Socrates' last words mean that he wanted his doctor's bill paid off. Others have put forward a more ingenious metaphysical explanation. An alternative translation of Socrates' last words reads: "Crito, we ought to sacrifice a cock to Asclepios. See to it, and don't forget." Asclepios's powers were said to include the ability to heal one's soul of the ills of this world, in preparation for the next. So Socrates' gift of a chicken may well have been in the hope of a safe passage for his soul to the next world. This would be in line with his belief in the immortality of the soul. As Socrates explained to his gathered friends before he drank the hemlock: "Only those who have lived an evil life hope that death is the end of everything for them. This is perfectly reasonable, for it is in their interests that it should be so. However, I am convinced that the souls of the wicked wander desolately through the lower world of Tartarus. Only those who have lived good lives will be admitted to the Real World." Socrates was man enough (and philosopher enough) to admit an element of uncertainty on this point. Before drinking the hemlock, he announced to his friends: "We go our separate ways—I to die, and you to live. Which one is better God alone knows."

Within days of Socrates' death the people of Athens realized the enormity of what they had done. A period of mourning for Socrates was declared. Gymnasia, theatres, and schools were closed. Meletus was condemned to death, and Anytus was banished. Later a bronze statue of Socrates by Lysippus was erected on the Sacred Way—somewhere for the unemployed to gather beneath their noblest protagonist.

This is all very honorable and would appear to reflect well on the citizens of Athens. But to me it suggests that Socrates was merely a pawn in some deeper political contest. In the overall game Socrates as usual won hands down—or we wouldn't be reading about him today.

Afterword

The Elusive Socrates

We know about Socrates from two main sources —Plato and Xenophon, both of whom were pupils of Socrates. Plato went on to become a philosopher, recording his philosophy in his masterly dialogues, a large number of which feature Socrates. Xenophon, on the other hand, became a soldier whose military career was such a disaster that he turned to writing instead. One of his best-known works is his *Memorabilia*, which describes Socrates.

Unfortunately these two firsthand sources present us with two different pictures of Socrates, which only occasionally overlap. Xenophon was conservative by nature and was outraged that his old teacher should be accused of corrupting the youth of Athens. His defensive portrayal of Socrates contains a wealth of anecdotal detail but very little actual philosophy. Indeed, sometimes Socrates scarcely appears to be a philosopher at all. In one of Xenophon's dialogues, *Oeconomicus*, Socrates turns up as a character—but is mainly concerned with offering advice on how to look after a garden. And often in Xenophon's *Memorabilia*, Socrates' ideas are so boring and unoriginal that it is difficult to see what all the fuss over him was about. Such a man should certainly never have been prosecuted for preaching subversive ideas, but such a man was also never a great philosopher.

Xenophon may have been too dim to absorb Socrates' ideas, but he also gives the impression of being too dim to present an imaginative picture of Socrates that wasn't true. For this reason, many have been inclined to accept Xenophon's picture of Socrates. Bertrand Russell firmly disposes of this attitude: "A stupid man's report of what a clever man says is never accurate, because he unconsciously translates what he hears into something that he can understand."

Conversely, Plato's rendering of Socrates may have been too clever by half. The Socrates who emerges from Plato's dialogues is a masterfully drawn literary portrait. Here is a superb character but very much a work of art—prompting suspicion that it may well be an "improvement" on the original man (an "improvement" with artistic rather than moral intent—Plato's Socrates is no saint).

Likewise there is the difficulty of separating what Socrates actually said from what Plato *wanted* him to say. We know that Plato put much of his own philosophy into Socrates' mouth, but how much?

The picture of Socrates I have drawn is taken from both these sources. Where they overlap, one sometimes catches a glimpse of an unmistakable but unpredictable character. This is the elusive man I have tried to capture.

All are agreed that Socrates prided himself on a certain elusiveness both in his arguments and his personality. He may well have eluded us to this day.

The Legacy of Socrates

Socrates' heritage is an ambiguous one (as no doubt he would have wished it). His influence on Plato was profound, and as such has continued to permeate philosophy to this day. This ancient Greek legacy has been compared to garlic. Once it got into the dish, it was impossible to get it out. One taste of philosophy and its ancient Greek flavor continues to repeat itself, no matter what.

Socrates' dialectic proved decisive. This conversational method almost certainly dictated the literary form of Plato's great dialogues, but its effect on philosophy is difficult to exaggerate. Socrates' method of analyzing a subject was the first significant use of reason for its own sake in philosophy. He would begin by asking his adversary to define the subject under discussion—which might be anything from the nature of justice to the method of becoming a general. Whether sublime or ridiculous, the subject was given the same treatment. This was the great innovation of the dialectic: it was a tool that could be applied to anything. Having elicited a definition of the subject, Socrates would then proceed to pick holes in it, and in the process a better definition would be achieved. In this way he advanced from particular examples to those with more general application, finally arriving at the universal truth.

Such truths, and Socrates' method of arriving at them, were the forerunner of logic—which was to be invented in the following century by Aristotle, Plato's pupil. Aristotle too accepted the Theory of Forms, though he modified it to his own requirements. It was Aristotle who reawakened philosophy's interest in reality, reversing the trend established by Socrates and Plato. Aristotle tried to include everything in philosophy—from cosmology to conchology, from science to sin. But in the end his main success was in mapping out the territory of human knowledge. Once again the emphasis was on theory rather than on hard knowledge that could be developed for practical use. Consequently when the Romans conquered the Greeks, philosophy fell into decline. It was of no use, and thus of no use to the Romans.

The collapse of the Roman Empire was followed by the Dark Ages and the religion-dominated civilization of the Middle Ages. Philosophy remained moribund: a vacuum of abstraction, hermetically sealed within religious orthodoxy. The mental energy that created the most intricate, all-embracing, and profound theology the world has ever seen was capable in technological terms of inventing little more than the harness (whose mechanics had already been foreseen in the third century B.C. by Archimedes). Gothic cathedrals arose amidst hovels lining streets of open sewers, and plagues were combatted with superstition.

This was not Socrates' fault, but the turn our thinking took as a result of his philosophy played a significant part. Human learning owes Socrates an immeasurable debt. He showed us *how* to use reason. But at the same time he limited our vision of *where* to use it. As a result, human learning was to suffer from a colossal blind spot. This lasted for no less than *three-quarters* of the period from the beginnings of philosophy to the present day.

An example of this black spot is to be seen in the medieval attitude to the Black Death, the plague that wiped out more than half the population of Europe in the fourteenth century. The Black Death was known to be contagious from the very start. (The disease arrived in the West after plague-ridden corpses were catapulted into a besieged Genoese trading post on the Black Sea.) Yet this *practical* knowledge was largely ignored in favor of spiritual measures. Why? Because logic—the successor to Socrates' dialectic —was habitually applied to *abstract* ideas, not practical matters. As we have seen, this blind spot is recognizable in Socrates. But he should not be blamed for the enormity of its later consequences (the virtual cessation of human advance). We all make mistakes, even if we are great philosophers. We just don't expect to see them perpetuated for almost two thousand years.

Some Observations Attributed to Socrates

As Socrates wrote nothing down, it seems only fair to begin with a quotation that explains why he did this:

Knowing nothing, what *could* I write down?

He goes on to explain:

Once there was an ancient Egyptian god called Theuth. He invented numbers, geometry, astronomy, dice, and writing. One day Theuth went to see Thamus, the King of Upper Egypt, and began to show him all he had invented.

When Theuth reached the alphabet, he explained: "This is an invention which will greatly improve the wisdom and memory of your people." But the king replied: "O ingenious Theuth, your alphabet will have exactly the opposite effect from the one you claim. As soon as Egyptians begin to rely upon written wisdom, they will stop using their memory and call things to mind not by using their own internal resources, as they should, but by using these external signs."

—Plato, *Phaedo*, 274, 275

After referring to his mother, who was a midwife, Socrates explains his philosophical method, likening it to her work:

The obstetrics which I practice is the same as that of all midwives, except that they practice on women, while I do so on men. They deal with the body, and I deal with the mind. . . . I myself am empty of wisdom, which is why the god

Apollo makes me attend to the wisdom of others, and prevents me from giving birth myself.
—Plato, *Theaetetus*, 149a, 150c

A Few Quips and Anecdotes

The unexamined life is not worth living.
—Plato, *Apology*, 38a

Dear Agathon, it is truth you cannot contradict. You can easily contradict Socrates.
—Plato, *Symposium*, 201d

A foreigner who knew about faces once passed through Athens. When he encountered Socrates, he told him straightaway that he was a monster, that within him he harbored all manner of vices and evil desires. Socrates merely replied: "You know me, sir!"
—Quoted by Nietzsche, *Twilight of the Idols*, The Problem of Socrates

Someone asked Socrates whether he should get married or not, and received the reply: "Do as you please, since whatever you do you will regret it."

—Diogenes Laertius, *Lives of the Eminent Philosophers*, II, 3

Socrates at Work

Once more Aristippus asked Socrates if he knew anything beautiful. He replied, "Many things."

"Do they all resemble each other?" inquired Aristippus.

"Some of them are as unlike each other as it is possible to be."

"But how can what is beautiful be unlike what is beautiful?"

Socrates replied: "Because one man who is beautifully formed for wrestling is likely to be different from another who is formed for running. And a shield that is beautifully formed for defense is as unlike as possible to a dart that is beautifully formed for being aggressively and swiftly hurled."

—Xenophon, *Memorabilia of Socrates*, VIII, 4

Socrates, at his trial, explains the reason for his unpopularity. He recalls that the Delphic Oracle, which speaks for the god Apollo, once pronounced him the wisest among men:

When I heard of this, I said to myself: What can the God mean? for I knew I had no wisdom. And yet I also knew the God did not lie. After meditating for a while on this question, I decided to see if the pronouncement of the God could possibly be true. If I could just find one man who was wiser than myself, then I could refute the God. So I went along to see someone who had the reputation of being wise. I need not mention his name: he was a politician, and the result of our meeting was as follows. When I started talking with him, I couldn't help thinking that he wasn't really very wise at all, although he was thought wise by many, and thought even wiser by himself. Thereupon I tried to explain to him that he only thought he was wise, but wasn't really wise at all. As a result he hated me, and this enmity was shared by several people who were present and heard what I had said. So I left him, saying to myself as I went: Well, although I don't suppose either of us knows anything really beautiful and good, I am better off than he is, for he knows nothing and thinks that he knows something; I neither know nor think that I know anything. It looks as if perhaps I *do* have a slight advantage over him. Then I went to another, who had still higher pretensions to wisdom, and my conclusion was exactly the same. Whereupon I made another enemy. . . .

—Plato, *Apology*, Chap. 6

Socrates, on the morning of his death in his condemned cell, speaks with his gathered friends of the soul, truth, and immortal wisdom:

It appears there is a narrow path which brings us safely to our journey's end, with reason as our guide. As long as we have a body, and this evil can mingle with our soul, we shall never completely attain what we desire, namely truth. For the body is forever wasting our time with its demands. Whenever it is ill it hinders us in our pursuit of real being. It fills us with passions, desires, fears, and all kinds of imaginings and foolishness. It is always preventing us from thinking properly. The body alone, and its desires, cause wars, social divisiveness, and battles: for the origin of all war is the desire for wealth, and we are forced to pursue wealth because we are enslaved by the wishes of the body. On account of all this, we have no leisure for philosophy. Even if we manage to free ourselves from the body for a while, and try to examine some matter, it hinders us at every step of our inquiry, causing confusion and trouble and panic, so that we cannot see the truth for it. Truly we have learned that if we are to have any pure knowledge at all we must be freed from the body. The soul by itself can see things as they truly are. Only after we are dead, it seems, can we gain the wisdom that we desire and for which we claim to have a passion. But this cannot happen while we are alive, as my argument shows. For if it is impossible to have pure knowledge while we have a body, one of two things must be true: either we can never gain any true knowledge, or we can only gain it after we are dead. For then, and only then, will the soul exist by itself, separate from the body. While we live we come closest to true knowledge if we have no use for or communion with the body beyond what is absolutely necessary, and if we are not defiled by its nature. We must live pure of the body until God releases us. When we are thus pure and released from the follies of the body we shall dwell, I imagine, with others who are pure like ourselves, and we shall of ourselves know all that is pure.

—Plato, *Phaedo*

Already it is time for us to part—for me to die, for you to continue living. Whichever of us takes the better course is unknown to anyone but God.

—Plato, *Apology*, 42a

70

Chronology of Significant Philosophical Dates

6th C B.C.	The beginning of Western philosophy with Thales of Miletus.
End of 6th C B.C.	Death of Pythagoras.
399 B.C.	Socrates sentenced to death in Athens.
c 387 B.C.	Plato founds the Academy in Athens, the first university.
335 B.C.	Aristotle founds the Lyceum in Athens, a rival school to the Academy.

324 A.D.	Emperor Constantine moves capital of Roman Empire to Byzantium.
400 A.D.	St. Augustine writes his *Confessions*. Philosophy absorbed into Christian theology.
410 A.D.	Sack of Rome by Visigoths heralds opening of Dark Ages.
529 A.D.	Closure of Academy in Athens by Emperor Justinian marks end of Hellenic thought.
Mid-13th C	Thomas Aquinas writes his commentaries on Aristotle. Era of Scholasticism.
1453	Fall of Byzantium to Turks, end of Byzantine Empire.
1492	Columbus reaches America. Renaissance in Florence and revival of interest in Greek learning.
1543	Copernicus publishes *On the Revolution of the Celestial Orbs*, proving mathematically that the earth revolves around the sun.

1633	Galileo forced by church to recant heliocentric theory of the universe.
1641	Descartes publishes his *Meditations*, the start of modern philosophy.
1677	Death of Spinoza allows publication of his *Ethics*.
1687	Newton publishes *Principia*, introducing concept of gravity.
1689	Locke publishes *Essay Concerning Human Understanding*. Start of empiricism.
1710	Berkeley publishes *Principles of Human Knowledge*, advancing empiricism to new extremes.
1716	Death of Leibniz.
1739–1740	Hume publishes *Treatise of Human Nature*, taking empiricism to its logical limits.
1781	Kant, awakened from his "dogmatic slumbers" by Hume, publishes *Critique of Pure Reason*.

	Great era of German metaphysics begins.
1807	Hegel publishes *The Phenomenology of Mind*, high point of German metaphysics.
1818	Schopenhauer publishes *The World as Will and Representation*, introducing Indian philosophy into German metaphysics.
1889	Nietzsche, having declared "God is dead," succumbs to madness in Turin.
1921	Wittgenstein publishes *Tractatus Logico-Philosophicus*, claiming the "final solution" to the problems of philosophy.
1920s	Vienna Circle propounds Logical Positivism.
1927	Heidegger publishes *Being and Time*, heralding split between analytical and Continental philosophy.
1943	Sartre publishes *Being and Nothingness*, advancing

Heidegger's thought and instigating existentialism.

1953   Posthumous publication of Wittgenstein's *Philosophical Investigations*. High era of linguistic analysis.

Chronology of Socrates' Life

469 B.C.	Socrates born just outside Athens.
Before 440 B.C.	Delphic Oracle pronounces Socrates "the wisest of men."
Circa 430 B.C.	Socrates serves as hoplite (common soldier) in the Peloponnesian War and saves life of Alcibiades at battle of Potidaea.
423 B.C.	Socrates parodied in comedy by Aristophanes.
Circa 420 B.C.	Marries Xanthippe. During the ensuing decade they have three sons.

406–405 B.C.	Serves as member of the legislative council (Boule).
404 B.C.	Refuses Thirty Tyrants' order to arrest Leon.
399 B.C.	Charged with impiety and corruption of youth. Trial of Socrates, which ends in him being sentenced to death. Takes judicial hemlock and dies.

Chronology of Socrates' Era

460s B.C.	Aeschylus, the first classical tragic dramatist, at the height of his powers.
460 B.C.	Outbreak of First Peloponnesian War between Athens and Sparta. Birth of Hippocrates, the traditional founder of medicine, on the island of Kos.
445 B.C.	End of First Peloponnesian War.
Mid-440s B.C.	Beginning of golden era in Athens under rule of Pericles. During this period Athenian culture flourishes at its greatest.

447 B.C.	Construction of the Parthenon begins on the Acropolis at Athens.
441–440 B.C.	Revolt of Samos breaks peace in the Aegean.
431 B.C.	Outbreak of Second (Great) Peloponnesian War between Sparta and Athens.
429 B.C.	Death of Pericles.
428 B.C.	Death of Anaxagoras, first Athenian philosopher, teacher of Socrates and Pericles.
415 B.C.	Athens launches great expedition to conquer Sicily, which ends in disaster.
404 B.C.	Second Peloponnesian War ends in humiliating defeat of Athens. Thirty Tyrants take power in Athens.
403 B.C.	Thirty Tyrants deposed and democracy restored.
400 B.C.	Reform of the laws and general amnesty (which does not apply, a year later, to Socrates).

Recommended Reading

Hugh H. Benson, *Essays on the Philosophy of Socrates* (Oxford University Press, 1992)

Thomas C. Brickhouse and Nicholas D. Smith, *Plato's Socrates* (Oxford University Press, 1993)

Scott Buchanan, ed., *The Portable Plato* (Viking, 1977)

William K. Guthrie, *Socrates* (Cambridge University Press, 1977)

Paul A. Vander Waerdt, ed., *The Socratic Movement* (Cornell University Press, 1994)

Index

A NOTE ON THE AUTHOR

Paul Strathern has lectured in philosophy and mathematics and now lives and writes in London. A Somerset Maugham prize winner, he is also the author of books on history and travel as well as five novels. His articles have appeared in a great many publications, including the *Observer* (London) and the *Irish Times*. His own degree in philosophy was earned at Trinity College, Dublin.

NOW PUBLISHED IN THIS SERIES:

Plato in 90 Minutes
Aristotle in 90 Minutes
Descartes in 90 Minutes
Kant in 90 Minutes
Nietzsche in 90 Minutes
Wittgenstein in 90 Minutes
Socrates in 90 Minutes
St. Augustine in 90 Minutes
Kierkegaard in 90 Minutes
Hegel in 90 Minutes

IN PREPARATION:

Thomas Aquinas, Bacon, Berkeley,
Confucius, Hume, Leibniz, Locke,
Machiavelli, Marx, J. S. Mill, Bertrand
Russell, Sartre, Schopenhauer, Spinoza